The Prestige S

Yorkshire Wo

John Banks

Photography by G H F Atkins

© 2000 J M Banks & G H F Atkins
ISBN 1 898432 28 7

Cover: A simple dark-red and cream livery and a restrained fleetname transfer in the traditional style grace No. **856** (**EHD970**), a 1960 Harrington-bodied AEC Reliance 41-seater seen at Coventry in June 1964.

Rear cover: An equally fine livery, with the colour proportions reversed, is evident on Leyland AN68 Atlantean No. **773** (**MUA870P**) of 1976, photographed at Leeds in September 1978. But this is not what it might seem. At that date National Bus Company corporate liveries held almost universal sway. Number 773 had been repainted in a version of the traditional livery to celebrate the 75th anniversary of the Company. The vehicle was repainted to standard after about 18 months.

Title page: In those of this series of books which celebrate the magnificent G H F Atkins Collection little has been said, primarily for space reasons but also because of the photographer's innate modesty, about the technical mastery evident throughout. Unlike many another photographer, Geoffrey Atkins is not afraid of exposing negatives in dull conditions, during showers of rain, when snow is on the ground, in fog or at night (all of which have appeared in this series). He is also perfectly happy to take a shot straight into the sun, with astonishingly forward results. This Sovereign Street, Leeds view of July 1951 stars Yorkshire Woollen's 1951 Leyland Olympic No. **688** (**HD8542**) with, in the background, 1948's Leyland Titan PD2/1 No. **547** (**HD7830**).

Opposite page: The Guy Arab came to many fleets during the Second World War and more often than not remained in a minority. Such was its personality, however, that a picture of an Arab can often be characteristic of a fleet, particularly when, as so often happened, further examples were added after the war. This one is Yorkshire Woollen's 1947 Northern Coachbuilders-bodied 56-seater No. **529** (**HD7812**) at Huddersfield in November 1953.

Below: Handsome Windover-bodied coaches featured regularly on Yorkshire Woollen's express operations. Number **726** (**HD8593**), a Leyland Tiger PS2/3, was on such work passing through Woodthorpe, Nottingham in July 1952.

INTRODUCTION

The old registration letter system in the United Kingdom was very much a part of youthful enthusiasms for matters transport. The family car, a 1930s Ford 8 registered DRH179, was locally registered. So were the writer's local bus fleets of Hull Corporation and East Yorkshire, with AT, KH and RH index marks, and they were easy to follow once one had worked out the order in which the registrations were issued. More distant operators were less easy, with London Transport the epitome of confusion for the youthful enthusiast in his provincial fastness. Some fleets, however, appeared to have all their new deliveries in a single registration series. United Automobile Services, for example, were all HN after 1933; United's westerly alter ego, Crosville, used the FM sequence. Midland Red had HA, Yorkshire Woollen District HD, Yorkshire Traction HE and West Riding HL. There was an added attraction to the recording of such fleets because of this numerical homogeneity, and how odd that so many of them began with H. Many municipal fleets were characterised by a single mark; two of them (Doncaster - DT, Rotherham - ET) were adjacent to the HD, HE and HL company areas

This neatness was occasionally sullied by the acquisition of second-hand vehicles and in 1974 the whole system was thrown into confusion. The task of vehicle registration was taken away from the County and County Borough Councils, which themselves were comprehensively reorganised, was transferred to the computerised system based at Swansea, and administered through newly created Local Vehicle Licensing Offices. Those changes are still widely regretted by many. In this book, the vehicles of the Yorkshire Woollen company are characterised by the constancy of the HD registrations, and its loss was one of the features that marked the end of the classic period.

Yorkshire Woollen... Why "*Woollen*"? Geography lessons (not among the favourites) at school partly answered the question. Time was when the woollen industry of Britain, nay of the world, was to be found concentrated into a district of the West Riding of Yorkshire. The principal cities and towns which made this great industry were Leeds and Bradford, Halifax, Huddersfield and Wakefield, arranged in a circle hardly twenty miles across and each concentrating on one aspect of the woollen industry. The sixth notable woollen town was

Dewsbury, in the centre of the circle. From the foothills in the east to the high Pennines in the west, it was significant that in this hilly territory were to be found both sheep and fast-flowing water. From the earliest days water was important in the woollen manufacturing processes, but as the industry developed the water came to drive the machinery in the factories, and to provide a route via the Rivers Aire and Calder to Hull for the export of finished cloth. A vivid image of the growth of the woollen industry in these parts is to be found in *Shirley*, one of the stunning classic novels of Charlotte Brontë (1816-1855), who from her schooldays here had many connections with the immediate district. The story is set in 1811-12 and features "Hollow's Mill" in a typical little valley. *"The other day I passed up the Hollow, which tradition says was once green, and lone, and wild; and there I saw the manufacturer's day-dreams embodied in substantial stone and brick and ashes - the cinder-black highway, the cottages, and the cottage gardens; there I saw a mighty mill, and a chimney ambitious as the tower of Babel."*

The growth of a plethora of small mill towns with resounding names like Heckmondwike and Cleckheaton, as well as the more prosaic Batley and Mirfield, created a populous industrial area. Today we look at the blackened mill buildings, now put to a variety of other uses, and countless stone houses, shops, churches and other buildings strongly characteristic of this particular area. They are augmented on an ever increasing scale by the more modern buildings and motorways which are the same everywhere. Yet with a little imagination we can look back two centuries with Charlotte Brontë, and then we can view the teeming Woollen District as it was a hundred years ago, when the steam trams of the Dewsbury, Batley & Birstal (sic) company were about to be replaced by the electric cars of the Yorkshire (Woollen District) Electric Tramways Company, a BET subsidiary registered on 19th November 1901. The first YWD electric tram route opened in February 1903.

The two principal lines from Dewsbury, to Batley and Birstall and to Heckmondwike and Liversedge, were double track, but there were several other lines that were single with passing loops. These included the unconnected and separately owned line from Dewsbury to Ossett where it met the West Riding company's tracks from Wakefield. There were complex arrangements involving the various local

The Yorkshire Woollen District operating area as it stood in 1955 reveals a compact system based on Dewsbury. Adjacent operators such as Yorkshire Traction at Barnsley and West Riding at Wakefield, the municipal fleets at Huddersfield, Halifax, Bradford and Leeds, and a wide variety of smaller independents, all combined to make the West Riding of Yorkshire an enthusiast's paradise, particularly when contrasted with, say, Norwich, where neighouring operators were few and distant.

authorities, but the YWD company had built up a sizeable fleet of 69 cars by 1905, all four-wheelers and mostly double-deckers which were soon fitted with covered tops. Bus services augmenting the tramways were introduced as early as 1913, and expanded rapidly in the 1920s. For example, a through service between Huddersfield and Leeds was inaugurated in 1925, and express services began in 1929 with the company's participation in the Limited Stop service between Manchester and Newcastle. Buses had been virtually forced upon the Company because the adjoining Bradford and Huddersfield systems were built to non-standard gauges (different from one another and

neither the same as Yorkshire Woollen's). The Company's Ravensthorpe terminus and Huddersfield's Bradley terminus were connected by a motor bus service in 1913 which ran for about eight years and for a further period in the mid-1920s. The twenties saw other bus routes established and towards the end of the decade the abandonment of the trams was considered. In 1929 the London, Midland & Scottish and the London & North Eastern railways acquired jointly a fifty percent stake in Yorkshire Woollen.

Between 1932 and 1934 the company replaced its own tramway services as well as that of the Dewsbury & Ossett undertaking, and

This scene on the Dewsbury setts is redolent of coach holidays of the 1930s. Dewsbury's industry had closed down for the holiday week and there were so many passengers and coaches (there were at least another ten behind No. 326) to carry them that a policeman was required to control the crowds and the traffic, although here, in the early morning, he seems to have had little to do and his busiest work lay ahead of him. There are some wonderful cameos here: the fashionably dressed lady regarding the policeman, perhaps in conversation with him; the suited and bowler hatted (despite the bright sunshine) gentleman placing his suitcase on the pavement; his hatted and befurred wife; the Yorkshire Woollen driver in earnest conversation with someone just out of the picture... They all combine to evoke an era long vanished and unlikely ever to return. YWD No. 326 (HD5606) was a 1935 Leyland TS7 Tiger with Roe 32-seat front-entrance bus bodywork. The vehicle lasted in the fleet until 1949. (Photograph: Senior Transport Archive)

in 1935 the 'Tramways' was dropped from the title in favour of the name Yorkshire Woollen District Transport Company. Continued expansion brought the fleet to 282 by 1962, and a variety of jointly-operated services brought the company's buses to Sheffield and Manchester and its coaches to Liverpool, Coventry and London.

The Yorkshire Woollen District operating area was among the more mysterious to the writer in his youth. Sightings from the family car on weekend outings were few and far between and only added to the mystery. The fleet name YORKSHIRE was similar in style to that of EAST YORKSHIRE and the youthful observer thought that there must have been a connection. There was, of course, as they were both BET companies, but that was unknown at the time. In those days much was done by

instinct. There was not the wealth of monthly publications and enthusiast-orientated books that fill the shops today.

One day in, perhaps, 1952 I was out train spotting in Hull. It was a foggy day and there was some difficulty in reading cabside locomotive numbers on the area's dirty, scruffy freight engines. I recall seeing, from the street below, what I thought was an austerity 2-10-0 stopped at signals up on an embankment near Beverley Road bridge. I hadn't seen such an engine before and was mortified that I could not read its number in the fog. In desperation I shouted up to the footplatemen, "What's the number of your engine, please?" There was no answer.

I tell the story because it describes the same sort of frustrated enthusiasm that befell me one day when I was out on my bike in Hull doing

TIMETABLE

JUNE 1966

YORKSHIRE

WOOLLEN DISTRICT TRANSPORT CO. LTD.
INCORPORATING COUNTY MOTORS (LEPTON) LTD.

PRICE ONE SHILLING

Rusted staples - the bane of timetable collectors - are very evident in an otherwise complete and unworn Yorkshire Woollen District June 1966 issue. The "Incorporating County Motors (Lepton) Ltd." statement refers to a situation which originated in 1929 when YWD, jointly with Yorkshire Traction and West Riding, acquired an interest in County, which maintained its identity until, in the National Bus Company era, it was absorbed into the Yorkshire Traction operation. (Ken Braithwaite Collection)

Pedalling merrily from one BRS depot to another, I saw pass the top of the street, dishearteningly distant, a single-decker with the word "Yorkshire" on the side. I frantically chased after it, came close enough to see that it was HD-registered and was rather fed up as it gradually pulled away at a stately 21 miles per hour, about 19 mph being all that I could manage on my push-bike.

Could I have overtaken that vehicle, I had no camera and so could not have photographed it. Geoffrey Atkins, born in and a lifelong resident of Nottingham, was better placed in his youth when he began to see and photograph Yorkshire Woollen vehicles on express services passing through Nottingham's Huntingdon Street bus station on the way to and from London and Birmingham. Most of Geoffrey's prewar YWD pictures, in fact, were taken in Nottingham and it was not until the postwar period that visits to Leeds, Dewsbury, Barnsley and Huddersfield began to produce a record of the service bus fleet in its working environment.

Readers of earlier volumes in the *Prestige Series* will know that Geoffrey Atkins has a strong interest in the art of the coachbuilder and that many of his photographs were taken in pursuit of that interest. The writer was one of the worst of the breed of the "if it's there, photograph it" school. Even today forlorn attempts to acquire at least one picture of every bus in favourite fleets continue. This is not Geoffrey's way of working. He is first and foremost a selective photographer who deals with the entire process himself. Types of film and grades of paper are carefully chosen, as are items of hardware. Added to this is, of course, considerable skill both behind the lens and in the darkroom.

Thus we have, as we have had with the other fleets dealt with in this series, a fine procession of portraits committed to film from the early 1930s onwards of what was one of the

my Saturday morning survey of the local British Road Services depots, with whose foremen I had managed to establish a cautious working relationship. *"Yes, you can go and write down the numbers but if you get into any trouble in there I never saw you."* One day I climbed into the cab of an AEC Mammoth Major 8 and in so doing leant on the starter button. The engine fired. I couldn't switch it off and had to confess, thus becoming *persona non grata* at that particular yard for a week or two.

staunchest supporters of the Leyland *marque* in the country. Although Guy Arabs were perforce purchased during the war years and AEC gained a foothold in the mid-1950s, the salesmen from up near Preston could regard Yorkshire Woollen as one of their best and most faithful customers.

Yorkshire Woollen, unlike some of the other operators we have looked at in these books, was blessed with an operating area in which there was not much competition, and not many independents were bought out in the prewar period in comparison with that kind of activity elsewhere.

In the postwar years acquisitions were limited to coaching operators, three of whom were acquired between 1946 and 1960.

It would thus be difficult to find a more "neat and tidy" fleet. There had been some Daimlers in the pre-First World War period but Leylands appeared as early as 1922. Dennis Brothers of Guildford mounted a strong challenge in the mid-twenties, when many Model E chassis were supplied, but could not sustain the impetus in the face of the new Leyland range of Lions, Tigers and Titans.

Rather conveniently, one of the largest of the few prewar acquired fleets, that of G H Kilburn (Ideal Motors), Heckmondwike in 1929, was entirely Leyland, as had been the two buses from Box of Dewsbury in 1927. This good fortune continued in the 1930s when most of the small total of acquired vehicles were also Leylands. The Box of Dewsbury acquisition had been of stage services and in 1936 the Box coaching interests were acquired. These and other 1930s additions produced a few AECs and oddments on Star, Gilford, Karrier and Bedford chassis but there was really very little to disturb Leyland's ascendancy until the advent of the wartime Guy Arabs.

In 1968 the BET, which still controlled Yorkshire Woollen, sold its interests to the Transport Holding Company. The latter was in turn disbanded at the end of 1968 when the National Bus Company was created. Yorkshire Woollen and Hebble had been gradually merging during the late 1960s and in 1970 the YWD depot at Liversedge was transferred to Hebble along with Yorkshire Woollen's coaching services. Hebble's stage carriage services were at the same time split among Yorkshire Woollen, West Yorkshire and the Calderdale JOC.

From 1970 Yorkshire Woollen and the West Riding Automobile Company shared the same management team. Wakefield became the Head Office for both companies in 1971. Management of Hebble, now an exclusively coach-operating company, was transferred to National Travel in 1973.

Consequent upon the privatisation of the NBC, West Riding's management team mounted a successful buy-out in 1987. The new company was Caldaire Holdings. The name "Yorkshire Buses" was perpetuated as a trading name for the Dewsbury and Heckmondwike operations.

This newly found independence came to an end in 1995 when Caldaire sold out to British Bus. The latter's ownership did not last long as British Bus was acquired by the Cowie Group in 1996. At the end of 1997 Cowie announced that all its subsidiaries were to be adorned in a new corporate livery and to display a new corporate fleetname - Arriva - signalling the disappearance of all those long-familiar fleetnames including Yorkshire Woollen.

As always the writer acknowledges the help given by his good friends and stalwarts of the enthusiast world, Philip Battersby and Ron Maybray. Many authors' names appearing on book covers have behind them the expertise of others, never more so than in the case of this writer who has yet to stump the team of Philip and Ron on matters bus and coach. *The Prestige Series* is much in their debt.

Ken Braithwaite, Roy Marshall and David and Mary Shaw have kindly acted as proofreaders. The publications of The Omnibus Society and The PSV Circle have, as ever, been useful in the preparation of these background notes and the captions. The debt that enthusiasts owe to these organisations is immense and is here gratefully acknowledged.

Numerous discrepancies among items of research material - particularly concerning dates and seating capacities, but sometimes even of such fundamental data as coachbuilders - have become evident during the preparation of this book. In all such clashes, for the sake of consistency, the information contained in the PSV Circle publications has been preferred.

Finally, the usual disclaimer: this book is neither a history nor a fleet list of YWD - it is "merely" another selection from the peerless Geoffrey Atkins Collection.

John Banks
Romiley, Cheshire
October 2000

The Dennis Challenge

Geoffrey Atkins has never been a great collector of other photographers' work, preferring to set up and obtain his images of the coachbuilder's art by means of his own art. From time to time, however, aspects of a favourite operator's fleet escaped his personal attention, and then he did not hesitate to augment his collection with images from other sources. Yorkshire Woollen's Dennis Es of the mid-1920s were infrequent visitors to Nottingham during Geoffrey's early photographic activities, and in any case had been withdrawn by about 1932, and a number of official views were sought out to fill the gap. The view of No. **61** (**HD2980**) *(above)* is a rather fine evocation of a new 1927 Dennis E on the move through characteristic Woollen District scenery. The photograph was probably commissioned by the operator. It is not known for certain who built the body on No. 61; Ransomes or Brush seem likely contenders. Number **93** (**HD3431**) *(below)* was photographed at Loughborough Works by Brush themselves when the vehicle was new in 1928. These vehicles were old-fashioned in appearance (even then) but were purposeful, efficient and comfortable. They did not last the pace, though, and had gone within five or six years. Leylands only two or three years newer lasted well into the postwar period. *(Photographs: Geoffrey Atkins Collection)*

The Leyland Tiger

The Leyland TS1 was a revolution in more ways than one and operators were not slow to equip their fleets with it. The Tiger consigned many other makes to the ranks of the also-rans; even Gilford's splendid products could not survive after most of their customers were swallowed up by London Transport in 1933/4. Yorkshire Woollen was quick off the mark in 1928 with four 32-seat coaches. The coachbuilder is unknown. Whoever it was, their work lasted a mere four years for the quartet was rebodied by Weymann in May 1932 with 26-seat coach bodies. Number **88A** (**HD3440**) was the second. It is seen *(above)* in Parliament Street, Nottingham on a dismal December day in 1932 with Nottingham Corporation trams, buses and trolleybuses in the backbround. In the view below the same vehicle was at Huntingdon Street coach station, Nottingham in May 1933. On both occasions it was working the Harrogate to Birmingham express service, proudly proclaimed.

The Leyland Lion

The Lion was not far behind the Tiger in the Yorkshire Woollen fleet. There had been a pair of PLSC1s ex-Box of Dewsbury in 1927. New Lions were on the improved LT1 chassis in 1929 and 1930 with 30-seat bus bodywork by Leyland, Brush or Ransomes. The Brush version is represented by No. **152** (**HD4040**), seen *(above)* at Huntingdon Street, Nottingham in August 1933 bearing the unhelpful destination infomation "DUPLICATE CAR". Photographs of the Ransomes-bodied batch of six (153-158) are rare, for all were withdrawn before the war. Geoffrey Atkins did not see one and again resorted to a manufacturer's official view. Number **154** (**HD4076**) displays the rather bulbous design of the Ransomes coachwork in this 1930 view. *(Photograph of HD4076: Geoffrey Atkins Collection)*

Leyland Tigers in Mansfield Road

Geoffrey Atkins was an early advocate of pictures of vehicles in motion to leaven the otherwise unrelieved diet of posed pictures in bus stations. In his home town of Nottingham the obvious place for such experiments was Mansfield Road, up and down which a wide variety of buses and coaches, trams and trolleybuses ran. Many of the express services of out-of-town operators were among these, including the Yorkshire Services Pool, of which YWD was a partner. Roe-bodied 26-seat TS2 service bus, dating from 1931, No. **182 (HD4367)** *(above)* was on its way to Leeds in August 1935 and 1932's TS4 No. **231 (HD4677)**, a Weymann-bodied 26-seat coach photographed in March 1934, had the the full panoply of route boards for the Harrogate to Birmingham service.

<<< *Previous page:* One of the best of the Mansfield Road shots is this one of No. **232** (**HD4678**), the second of the 1932 Weymann-bodied 26-seat coaches, taken on the setts and tramlines in May 1935. There is a livery variation compared with that carried by No. 231 a year earlier *(see page 12)*. The service being worked was the Bradford to London and there is a splendid cameo of the second driver making his own air-conditioning.

This page: Ten Titan TD2s with Roe 48-seat centre-entrance bodies came in 1932. The last of them, No. **248** (**HD4810**) was withdrawn and sold to Williamson of Bridlington in 1948. It was seen *(above)* in Bridlington in June 1950, shortly before Williamson sold out to East Yorkshire. Leyland Cub No. **250** (**HD4902**), with Roe 20-seat bus bodywork, was a 1933 delivery. It was at Scarborough in June 1935.

Leyland Titans

A batch of nine Leyland TD3 Titans with Weymann centre-entrance 48-seat bodywork entered the Yorkshire Woollen District fleet in 1933. The first of them, No. **269** (**HD5041**), was photographed *(above)* by the bodybuilder before the vehicle was sent north to Dewsbury. Centre-entrance, 48-seat TD3s were also purchased in 1934. This time the Leeds coachbuilder Charles H Roe supplied the bodies. Four of them were rebodied by the same bodybuilder in the summer of 1948. The new bodies were 56-seaters with rear entrances, exemplified by No. **311** (**HD5354**), photographed at Queen Street, Leeds in April 1955. *(Photograph of HD5041: Geoffrey Atkins Collection)*

Roe Coachwork

The considerable visual difference caused by a redesigned radiator is clearly delineated in these views of 1933 Roe-bodied Leyland LT5 No. **257** (**HD4909**) *(above)* and the LT5A version, represented by the following year's No. **291** (**HD5208**) *(<<< opposite page)*. Number 257 was photographed when brand new and No. 291 was at Huntingdon Street, Nottingham in August 1935. *(Photograph of HD4909: Geoffrey Atkins Collection)*

In 1935 the first TS7 Tigers appeared in the YWD fleet. Roe again supplied the bodies for the 32-seat service bus version and there were two Weymann 26-seat coaches. Number **327** (**HD5607**) was at Glasgow Paddocks, Doncaster in April 1935.

August 1938, but a murky day nonetheless in this Huntingdon Street, Nottingham view. Number **373 (HD5829)**, a 1935 Roe-bodied 32-seat TS7 service bus, was duplicating No. **415 (HD6614)** on the express run to Bradford. Number 415 was a Tiger TS8 of 1938, and was thus brand new in this picture. Its 30-seat coachwork was by Duple.

Another of the 1935 TS7s. Number **397** (**HD6313**) in a classic GHFA portrait at Nottingham in August 1937.

The Leyland Tiger TS8

The TS8 - backbone of so many fleets from the late thirties onwards - appeared in the YWD fleet in 1938. There were both buses and coaches, the latter including three Duple-bodied 30-seaters, exemplified by No. **414** (**HD6613**) which was brand new when photographed *(<<< opposite page)* at Nottingham in August 1938. A rather gloomy Derby bus station view of August 1950 *(above)* includes No. **427** (**HD6802**), a 1939 TS8 with coachwork by Weymann, heading for Coventry via Birmingham. East Yorkshire's postwar Tiger No. **463** (**JAT431**) was alongside. Of the 10 Eastern Coach Works-bodied TS8 buses delivered to Yorkshire Woollen in 1938, five were rebodied as 30-seat coaches by Windover in 1949. Number **409** (**HD6608**), at Nottingham in August 1952 *(below)* demonstrates the very attractive combination of prewar chassis and postwar body.

22

The Leyland Titan TD5

The TD5 was to be seen in Yorkshire Woollen colours carrying either Roe or Eastern Coach Works bodywork. Number **451** (**HD6826**), seen at Queen Street, Leeds *(above)* in August 1949, was a 54-seat highbridge vehicle: Roe also supplied lowbridge bodies on the TD5. The ECW bodies, also highbridge, were a copy of the Roe design but were instantly recognisable by the protruding front destination indicator boxes. Numbers **454** (**HD7151**) *(below)* and No. **457** (**HD7154**) *(<<< opposite page)* were also at Queen Street in August 1949.

Wartime TS8s

Yorkshire Woollen's last vehicles to standard prewar specfication before the onslaught of war brought its manifold problems for operators all over the country were 22 Tiger TS8s with 32-seat Eastern Coach Works bus bodies delivered in 1940. All ran for exactly a decade and were withdrawn in 1950 although not sold until 1952. By 1940 Geoffrey Atkins's photography had become much reduced: service in the RAF claimed his attention and there was a shortage of film for hobby use. In the early postwar period as things began to return to something approaching normal, Geoffrey found and photographed two of the batch. Number **459 (HD7156)** was at Friar Lane, Nottingham *(above)* in May 1949, and No. **466 (HD7163)** was at Dewsbury in May 1950, presumably on a short working of the marathon Bradford to Sheffield service 66.

Most of the 1940 TS8s found new owners, including No. **475** (**HD7172**) which went to the Wimpey fleet on contract work. It is seen here in Nottingham in March 1955 surrounded by other fascinating vehicles including ex-Ribble and Rochdale double-deckers.

The Wartime Utility Buses

In 1942 Yorkshire Woollen managed to have allocated to it one Leyland Titan TD7 and one Guy Arab. The Titan was No. **480** (**HD7286**) which was fitted with Roe 56-seat bodywork. The vehicle was never rebodied and was withdrawn in 1954. It is seen *(above)* at Huddersfield in November 1953. In each of the years 1943 to 1947 only Guy Arabs were bought new. The earlier examples had austerity bodywork to Ministry of Supply specification from Weymann, Massey or Park Royal. The solitary 1942 example had been bodied by Duple. Number **498** (**HD7421**), seen at Dewsbury *(below)* in May 1954, was one of the Weymanns. Geoffrey missed the Guys with original bodywork and turned to a friend and fellow enthusiast for this picture. *(Photograph of HD7421: Roy Marshall)*

Guy Arabs

Most of Yorkshire Woollen District's wartime Guy Arabs were rebodied by Roe in the 1950s. Number **482** (**HD7308**) had been the first of a pair of Arab Is delivered in 1943 (they were followed by a pair of Arab IIs). It was rebodied in 1953 and was photographed soon afterwards *(<<< previous page)* at Dewsbury. As was so often the case, YWD found the Guy chassis, which would never have been purchased but for the exigencies of the war, to be solid, reliable and economical. Ten Arab IIs with Roe bodies were ordered in 1946, including No. **525** (**HD7658**), seen *(above)* in Leeds in August 1949. These were followed in 1947 by five Arab IIIs bodied by Northern Coachbuilders. Number **539** (**HD7822**) was in Huddersfield *(below)* in November 1953.

>>> *Opposite page:* A fine portrait of another of the Northern Coachbuilders Arab IIIs. Number **541** (**HD7824**) was at Dewsbury in May 1950.

Postwar Leyland Titans

Nineteen-forty-eight saw a return to Leyland for new chassis orders. The Loughborough coachbuilder Brush won the order to body batches of Titan PD2/1s and Tiger PS1s as service buses. For urgently needed new coaches, YWD commissioned six Duple-bodied PS1 32-seaters. The double-deckers in original condition are represented by Nos. **543 (HD7826)** *(above)* and **545 (HD7828)** *(<<< opposite page)*. They were respectively at Dewsbury garage in May 1954 and in Sovereign Street, Leeds in August 1949. Yorkshire Woollen, as did so many other operators for ease of spray painting, took the retrograde step in the mid-1950s of simplifying its livery. The traditional deep-red and cream gave way to a lighter, all-over red with no relief whatsoever. The result was visually unfortunate, as seen *(below)* on Brush-bodied Titan No. **554 (HD7837)** at Dewsbury in September 1955.

The Postwar Tigers

The 1948 single-deck service buses on Leyland PS1 chassis were 34-seaters from the Brush factory. Number **610** (**HD7893**), with anti-nationalisation advertising, was at YWD's Dewsbury garage *(above)* in May 1950. Sister vehicle No. **592** (**HD7875**) *(below)* features in an August 1949 photograph taken in Queen Street, Leeds.

Tiger Livery Variations

Above: Five of the 1948 Brush-bodied PS1s were repainted cream in the early 1950s. It is believed that they operated on summer seasonal work for Hebble Motor Services. Number **586 (HD7869)** was in Wellington Street coach station, Leeds in April 1955.

Below: The drab, unrelieved red also afflicted the single-deck fleet. This is another April 1955 Leeds view, in which No. **600 (HD7883)** was parked in Sovereign Street.

Variations on a theme

Above: Six of 1948's PS1 Tigers were 32-seat coaches bodied by Duple. Still quite new, No. **634** (**HD7992**) was at East Midland's Mansfield depot in May 1949. The six Duple coaches were later reseated to 33.

Below: Twenty-four of the 1948 PS1 service buses were rebodied as double-deckers in 1954/5. Metro-Cammell 56-seat bodies of "Orion" design were specified. The Orion was not among the most attractive of bodies and the all-over red livery did nothing to help. The unequal-height windows left acres of panelling which could have done with some cream relief. Number **562** (**HD7845**) was at Barnsley in June 1954.

Leyland Bodywork

Above: The 1949 batch of Leyland Titans had several features of interest. Numbers 639 - 646 were on the PD2/3 eight-feet-wide chassis with 56-seat highbridge Leyland bodywork. Number **645** (**HD8417**) was photographed at Dewsbury in May 1950. It had the original, traditional livery and an unusually large number of opening half-drop windows. The vehicle was one of a batch built for export, hence the extra opening windows. The batch was diverted to various BET companies.

Below: Exactly four years later, No. **640** (**HD8412**) was standing in the same spot on the same service G to Cleckheaton. Fewer opening windows are evident, as is the later, less attractive livery.

Roe-bodied Leyland Titans

<<< *Opposite page:* The 1950 Roe-bodied PD2/3 Titans were handsome vehicles. The highbridge 56-seat bodies were pleasing to the eye as well as functional and efficient. Number **672** (**HD8526**) features in a nostalgic scene in Dewsbury bus station in May 1950. The destination information for service C to Ravensthorpe (Fir Cottage) via Earlsheaton was very clear and readable.

This page: Numbers **652** (**HD8506**) *(above)* and **660** (**HD8514**) *(below)*, photographed in Queen Street, Leeds in May 1950 and in Huddersfield in May 1954, demonstrate the old and new liveries.

Windover coachwork

<<< Opposite page: The Windover concern supplied bodywork to a number of BET operators in the early postwar period. In 1949 and 1950 Yorkshire Woollen purchased a batch of eight Leyland Tiger PS2/3 chassis with 32-seat, front-entrance Windover bodies. Space was found for an extra seat (simply achieved by putting five instead of four across the long back seat) and all were 33-seaters by 1953. Number **686** (**HD8540**) was taking a break at Barnsley during an express run to Newcastle in August 1951.

This page: Two Derby bus station views - of No. **687** (**HD8541**) *(above)* and an unidentified example *(below)* - display the clean, unfussy lines of the Windover design, with its characteristic "leaning back" pillars and "teardrops". The pictures were taken in May 1951 and September 1953.

Willowbrook bodywork

Contemporaneously with Windover's fine coaches, another "W", Willowbrook, was supplying Yorkshire Woollen with 32-seat, front-entrance service buses on the very similar Leyland Tiger PS2/5 chassis. Taken in June 1950 during one of Geoffrey Atkins's memorable holidays in Scarborough, No. **697** (**HD8551**) *(<<< opposite page)* was waiting to leave for the resort of Bridlington, some 20 miles down the coast. In another Scarborough view *(above)*, this one from July 1953, No. **716** (**HD8570**) was in the cream livery applied to some of the batch. In a Barnsley bus station view *(below)* from September 1952, No. **700** (**HD8554**) was leaving on service 66 to Dewsbury. These vehicles were lengthened to 30 feet with six extra seats in 1955.

The Underfloor Engine Revolution

Underfloor engines were by no means new in the world of bus design at the turn of the decade from the 1940s to the 50s but that was when the concept began to revolutionise the bus and coach scene in Britain. Yorkshire Woollen tried both the Olympic and the Royal Tiger from the Leyland stable in 1951. On these two pages are examples of the Olympic when still very new. Number **736** (**HD9127**) was at Lower Mosley Street coach station, Manchester waiting to leave for Halifax in May 1952; and No. **735** (**HD9126**) was at Sovereign Street, Leeds on service 36 to Elland in August 1951.

Above: The previous year had seen a single underfloor-engined vehicle join the YWD fleet. Number **734** (**HD8970**) had been displayed at the 1950 Commercial Motor Show and was a Leyland Royal Tiger PSU1/13 with Brush 42-seat bodywork. Although it lasted until 1964 Geoffrey Atkins never managed to photograph No. 734 and so added this bodybuilder's official view to his collection. *(Photograph: Geoffrey Atkins Collection)*

Below and >>> opposite page: 1951's batch of Royal Tigers were very similar machines, again with Brush coachwork. Number **695** (**HD8549**), on a dull September day in 1955, was outside the YWD garage in Dewsbury. It had the all-red livery, relieved by a light band above the windows used for advertising Jubilee Stout. The original livery is seen on No. **694** (**HD8548**) at Dewsbury in May 1954.

Windover Coaches

The coach fleet was not neglected when underfloor-engined chassis were being ordered for 1951 delivery. Six Leyland Royal Tiger PSU1/15s with striking 30-seat, centre-entrance coachwork from Windover were specified. The batch was numbered 740-745 and Geoffrey Atkins found one each of the last two on different visits to Derby bus station in 1956. In January *(above)* No. **744** (**HD9152**), on a very dull day and rather grimy from the winter roads, was showing Newcastle as its destination. Number **745** (**HD9153**), rather cleaner but still suffering from dull weather, was going to Coventry in April *(below)*. The "teardrops" were a carry-over from Windover's coachwork for half-cab coaches but the window pillars were now vertical. The heavy appearance might perhaps have been lightened by fewer strips of side beading but the emblem incorporating the Company's fleetname on the front panel was an attractive feature.

Beadle Rebuilds

1952's only new vehicles were Nos. 746-755 which were Leyland-Beadle rebuilds incorporating mechanical parts from prewar Leyland TS7 or TS8 Tigers. The 35-seat coach bodies were built in-house by John C Beadle of Dartford. An attractive vehicle resulted at somewhat less than the cost of a brand new equivalent. The "teardrops", reminiscent of those on Windover coachwork seen in these pages, presented something of a styling problem on the nearside when the passenger sliding door was open. Number **750** (**HD9357**) *(above)* was at Dewsbury garage in September 1955 looking very smart. The last of them, No. **755** (**HD9362**), was at Derby bus station in October 1952 with another of the batch behind. They were going to Barnsley and Newcastle.

The Weymann Fanfare

For 1955/56 delivery Yorkshire Woollen gave the Weymann concern an order for twelve 39-seat coach bodies with front entrances to be mounted on AEC Reliance chassis. As if the move from Leyland to AEC were not dramatic enough, the red in the livery was a new, brighter shade and the registration number sequence changed from the original "HD" to "AHD", "BHD" and so on. The coaches in this batch, Nos. 756-767, were fitted with Weymann's Fanfare coachwork. One of them, No. 763 (BHD703), was illustrated on page 54 of the previous book in this series (*"Tyne-Tees-Mersey"*) where it was wrongly described as a Harrington Cavalier, for which error both authors and publisher apologise to readers. Our pictures here are of No **763 (BHD703)** accompanied by 1950's Windover-bodied Leyland Tiger No. **687 (HD8541)** at East Midland's Mansfield garage in September 1956 *(<<< opposite page),* and two views *(this page)* of No. **759 (AHD822)** at Derby bus station in May 1957. Number 763 was on seasonal holiday work to Brighton and No. 759 was on the express service to Newcastle upon Tyne.

Above: Nineteen-fifty-seven's coaches were perhaps even more out of the ordinary. Twelve front-entrance 41-seaters based on Commer running units were ordered from John C Beadle, of Dartford. In February 1958 at Derby bus station, in the gloomy weather which seemed to attend the photographer's efforts to record YWD vehicles at that location, No. **775 (CHD360)** was waiting to leave for Newcastle.

Below: In 1959 a return to AEC for chassis for single-deckers produced a batch of 22 vehicles with Park Royal 43-seat front-entrance bodywork. Our example is No. **821 (DHD201)**, photographed at Halifax in May 1959 whilst *en route* to Manchester. The high-backed seats, which nevertheless fell short of full coach specification, and cream livery perhaps indicated a "dual-purpose" rather than strictly service bus function.

AEC Double-deckers

Double-deckers on Leyland chassis had last been bought new in 1950: a large batch of PD2/3 Titans and an interesting half-dozen OPD2/1 models which had been built for, but never delivered to, Pretoria in SouthAfrica. Between then and 1957 the double-deck intake was catered for by borrowing Guy Arabs from Ribble Motor Services of Preston and from the East Kent Road Car Company of Canterbury, and having 24 Leyland Tigers dating from 1948 rebodied as double-deckers by MCCW in 1954/55. In the late nineteen-fifties and early sixties, having already moved to AEC for new single-deckers, Yorkshire Woollen turned to the AEC Regent V double-decker, first with MCCW Orion bodies, and then, in 1961, bodied by Northern Counties. In 1962 Leyland Titans once again featured in YWD's purchases. More single-deckers were rebodied as double-deckers in the 1960s, too, and then came the rear-engines revolution. MCCW-bodied AEC Regent V No. **66** (**DHD177**) dated from 1959 and had originally been numbered 797. The renumbering took place in 1967. The reappearance of some cream in the livery was welcome. The vehicle was withdrawn in 1971 and subsequently passed into preservation. Geoffrey Atkins found and photographed it at Wollaton Park, Nottingham in May 1992.

Coaches in the Early 1960s

<<< *Opposite page and above:* Here is the Harrington Cavalier-bodied AEC Reliance. These fine 41-seaters appeared in the Yorkshire Woollen fleet in 1960. In these views dating from August 1960 Geoffrey Atkins, whilst holidaying in Scarborough, found two of them on summer excursion work and photographed them using an orange filter to enhance the sky. Number **861** (**EHD975**) *(opposite page)* was south of Scarborough at Filey and No. **859** (**EHD973**) was further north at Whitby harbour.

Below: In 1961 a half-dozen Duple-bodied Ford 570Es appeared. This was a specification of coach more normally found in the independent sector. They lasted with YWD only until 1967. Number **871** (**GHD215**) was at Huntingdon Street, Nottingham in April 1963.

Longer Coaches

Above: 1962 saw a return to Leyland for coaches to the then new maximum length of 36 feet. Plaxton 49-seat coachwork was specified on Leopard chassis and the vehicles became the backbone of Yorkshire Woollen District's activities on the express services to London. Number **899** (**HHD346**) was passing through Woodthorpe, Nottingham in May 1964 heading for the Capital.

Below: In the archetypal Huntingdon Street coaching scene of the mid-1960s, No. **900** (**HHD347**), also bound for London, shares the limelight with East Midland's Alexander-bodied AEC Reliance No. **C266** (**266PRR**) and an East Yorkshire Willowbrook-bodied Leopard.

Above: Nineteen-sixty-five's Leyland Leopard Weymann 53-seaters had slightly more comfortable seats than had the standard service bus of the day, and were in cream and red livery when delivered and until about 1970. They were often found on longer-distance services, as exemplified by No. **954** (**AHD120B**) passing through Sherwood, Nottingham on the way to Leeds in August 1965.

Below: Number 949 (**AHD115B**) of the same batch - following its renumbering to 269 in 1967 and to 173 in 1971 - was withdrawn from passenger service in 1976 and used by Kirklees MDC as a canteen (with fleet number **A18**). It was later borrowed by the Trent Motor Traction Company for use as an enquiry office at Nottingham's Victoria bus station where it was photographed in February 1979. A power cable can be seen descending from on high and entering the vehicle's cab to provide mains electricity. The vehicle was back in Yorkshire Woollen's possession by 1981 and was sold to a dealer in 1982.

Leyland never regained the ascendancy it had enjoyed in the YWD fleet in the prewar and early postwar periods. When the Company eventually turned to rear-engined buses the Daimler Fleetline was chosen and although Leyland Atlanteans were ordered in 1967 there were also Fleetlines. Both types had Alexander bodywork seating 75. 1967's Fleetlines started a new numbering series. Number **9** (**DHD208E**) was brand new in this May 1967 shot in Barnsley bus station.

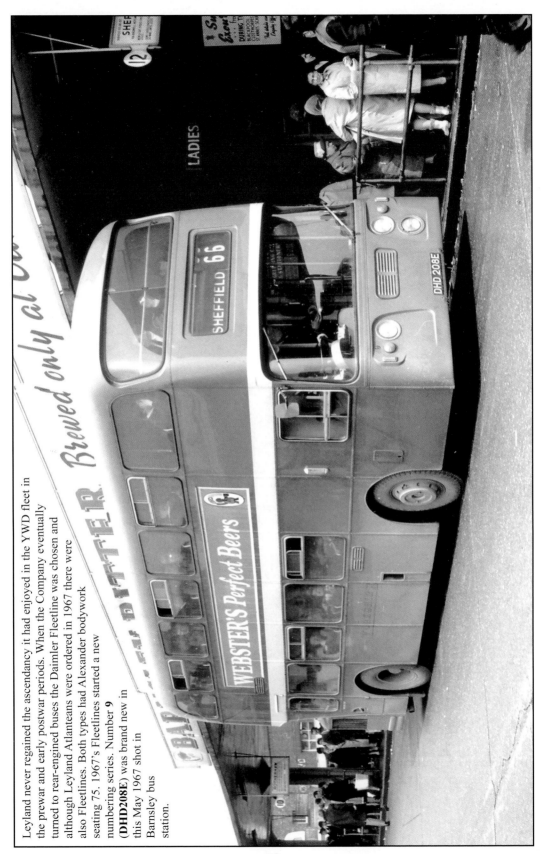

Plaxton Coaches

Above: In 1967 further Plaxton Panorama-bodied coaches were added to the fleet. The chassis were Leyland Leopards and there were both 41- and 45-seaters. Number **402 (DHD237E)**, a 45-seater, was at Huntingdon Street, Nottingham in December 1967 working an express service to Luton. Vehicles from the United Counties and Barton fleets can be seen on the left of the picture.

Below: On the same date and in the same place No. **404 (DHD239E)** of the same batch had clearly been driven through some very messy road conditions. It was also going to Luton and was apparently being duplicated by East Midland No. **C266 (266PRR)**, an AEC Reliance with Alexander coachwork.

<<< *Opposite page:* Alexander provided the coachwork for 1968's Leyland Leopards. These coaches joined the Plaxton-bodied examples on the express network. Number **409 (EHD524F)** was alongside a Trent double-decker at Huntingdon Street, Nottingham in September 1970. The positioning of the destination screen below the windscreen on this type of body altered the appearance considerably. The coach was bound for Birmingham.

Above: In a May 1969 view at Derby bus station No. **412 (GHD412G)** was going to Newcastle. One of five delivered in 1969, it was a 45-seat Alexander-bodied Leopard, described as "dual-purpose".

Below: Six Harrington-bodied centre-entrance 37-seat AEC Reliances dating from 1954/55 were bought from Maidstone & District Motor Services in 1968. Number **436 (TKM326)** was at Huntingdon Street, Nottingham in August 1969. These vehicles were short-lived in the YWD fleet and had gone by the end of 1970.

<<< Opposite page: The Leyland National, bland as it was, became the familiar "face" of many a fleet as the 1970s progressed. Yorkshire Woollen bought ten in 1972/3, one of which, No. **351 (MHD341L)**, was photographed in Aire Street, Leeds in June 1977.

Above: As the 1970s dawned YWD was still wedded to the Daimler Fleetline for new double-deckers. This was a time - the earliest years of the National Bus Company - when the fleet was being stocked with a ragbag of second-hand machinery from a variety of sources (including Bristol KSWs from United and West Yorkshire) and new buses were few. 1971, however, saw 11 Alexander-bodied Fleetlines delivered, of which No. 27 **(JHD327J)**, by then renumbered to **686**, was in Aire Street, Leeds in March 1979.

Below: When Eastern Coach Works products were once again generally available some interesting chassis/body combinations resulted. YWD bought 12 ECW-bodied 74-seat Daimler Fleetlines in 1972. Number **695 (LHD305K)** is seen in Sovereign Street, Leeds in March 1975.

<<< *Opposite page:* Number **773** (**MUA870P**), the 1976 Leyland Atlantean AN68/1R which was repainted in a special livery for the 75th anniversary of the Company, is seen turning out of Sovereign Street, Leeds in a remarkably quiet, traffic-free scene.

Above: From the same batch, Atlantean No. **769** (**MUA866P**) carries the normal National Bus Company colours and logos. The photograph was taken in Aire Street, Leeds in June 1977. We are now well into the era of the revised registration-issuing scheme which had resulted in 1974 in the loss of the "HD" series.

Below: The late 1970s are epitomised in this picture of an NBC-liveried Bristol VR. Number **783** (**RYG392R**) had been a 1977 delivery and was photographed in Sovereign Street, Leeds in September 1978.

...and a reminder of how it was...

Above: In a scene from about 1930/31 at the junction of Westborough and Valley Bridge Approach, Scarborough an amazing miscellany of public transport vies for attention: Scarborough trams, a 1927 United ADC service bus, a 1930 United Leyland Tiger coach, and a 1929 Yorkshire Woollen District Leyland Tiger TS1, with Roe 26-seat front entrance coach body, bringinging holidaymakers from the West Riding. Scarborough's trams were replaced by United buses on 1st October 1931. *(Photograph: Geoffrey Atkins Collection)*

Below: In the 1930s small buses often resembled large, luxurious private cars, as opposed to more modern examples which frequently look like (indeed, sometimes are) converted delivery vans. Number **252 (HD4904)** was a 1933 Leyland Cub photographed when new by Charles H Roe, who had built the body. *(Photograph: Geoffrey Atkins Collection)*